more favorite CLASSICS
ACCOMPANIMENT BOOK TWO

19 Favorite Pieces for
Late Intermediate through
Early Advanced Students
from the Four Stylistic Periods
~~of Piano Repertoire.~~

~~Sec~~ osed
~~Sec~~ Teacher,
~~Pa~~ ~~Advanced~~ Student.

Selected & Edited by E. L. Lancaster & Kenon D. Renfrow

About This Collection

The 19 pieces in this collection have proven to be favorites of late intermediate through early advanced students throughout the years. Chosen from the four stylistic periods of piano repertoire, the volume contains selections of varying difficulty levels so that it may be used over a two- to three-year period. Arranged in two-piano score format, the second keyboard part has been specially composed for a teacher, parent or more advanced student. The second keyboard part may be played on a second piano or electronic instrument and may also be recorded or sequenced to enhance practice, learning and performance.

A companion volume, *More Favorite Classics—Solo Book Two* (#32082), contains the original solo without the second keyboard part. The pieces in each collection have a page-by-page cross reference, and measures are numbered for ease of use.

Alfred Music Publishing Co., Inc.
P.O. Box 10003
Van Nuys, CA 91410-0003
alfred.com

ISBN-10: 0-7390-5874-6
ISBN-13: 978-0-7390-5874-9

Contents

Use with
MORE FAVORITE CLASSICS
Solo Book Two,
page 4.

Prelude in G Major

George Frideric Handel
(1685–1759)

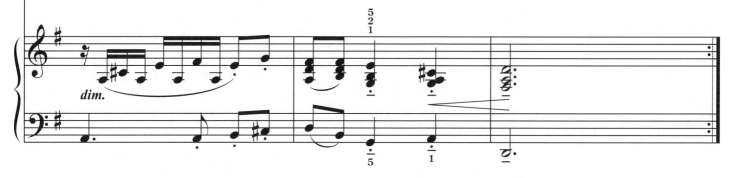

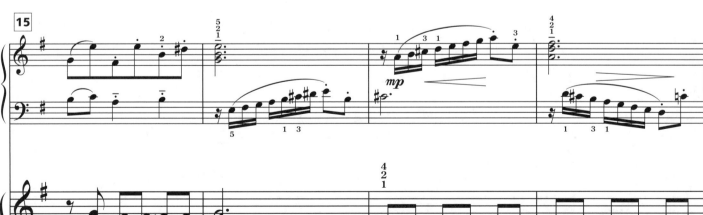

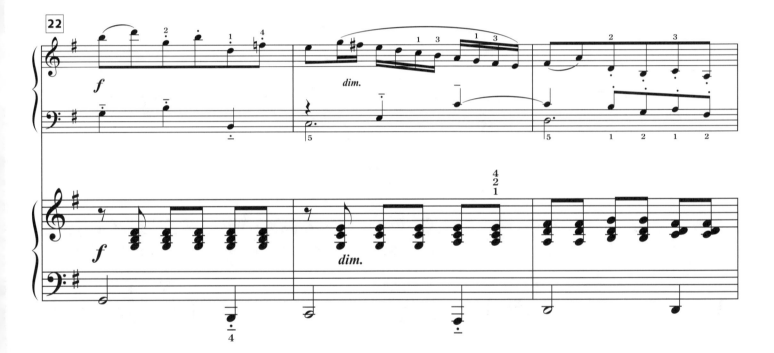

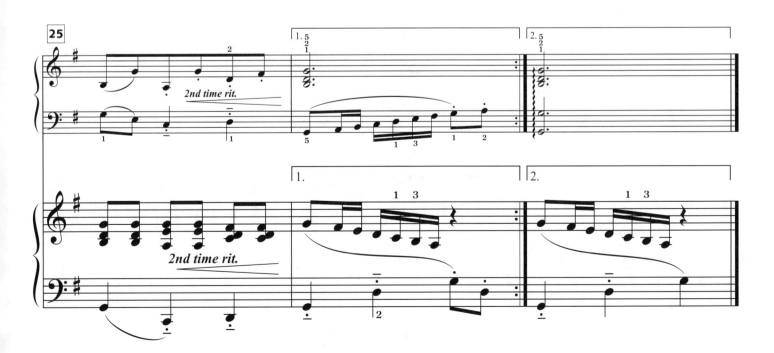

Invention No. 14 in B-flat Major

Johann Sebastian Bach (1685–1750)
BWV 785

* Play the eighth notes slightly detached throughout unless marked otherwise.

Gavotte
(French Suite No. 5 in G Major)

Johann Sebastian Bach (1685–1750)

BWV 816

* Play the quarter notes slightly detached throughout unless marked otherwise.

Use with
MORE FAVORITE CLASSICS
Solo Book Two,
page 10.

Little Prelude in C Major

Johann Sebastian Bach (1685–1750)
BWV 939

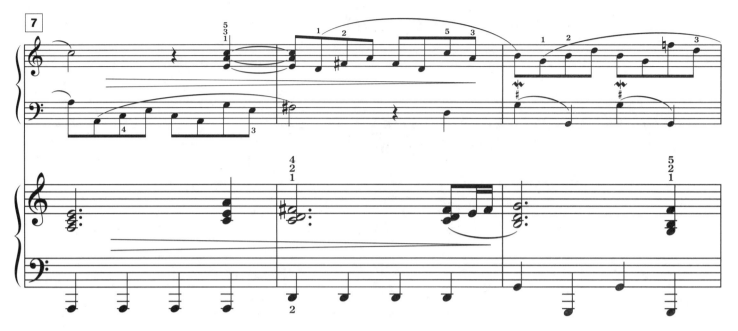

Use with
MORE FAVORITE CLASSICS
Solo Book Two,
page 11.

Für Elise

Ludwig van Beethoven (1770–1827)
WoO 59

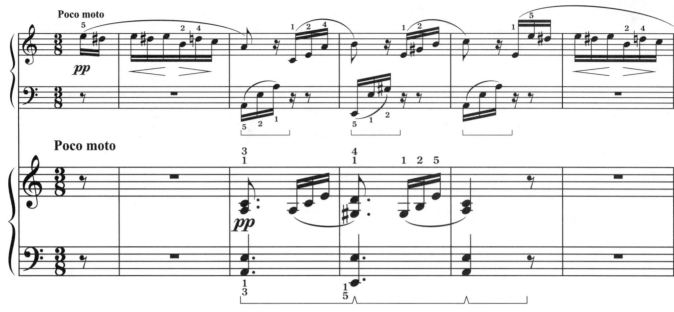

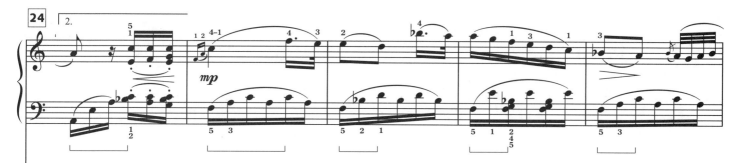

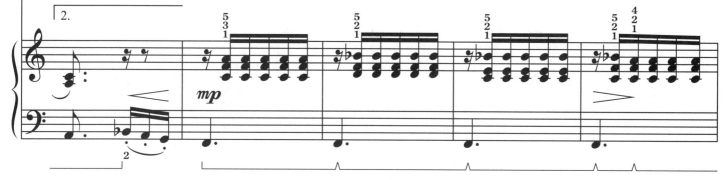

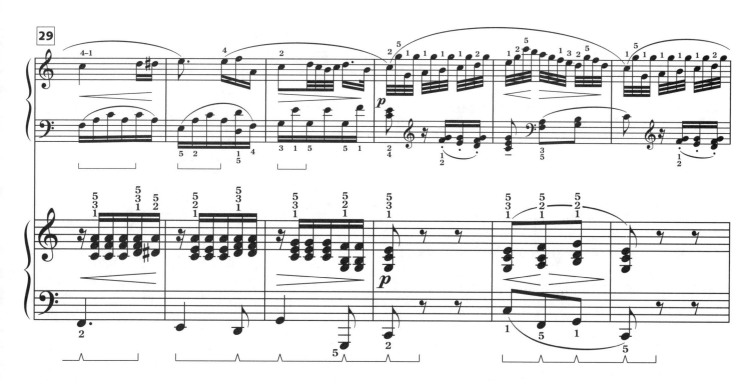

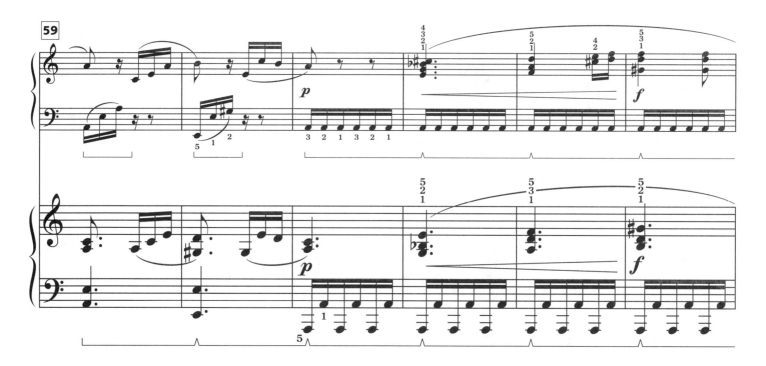

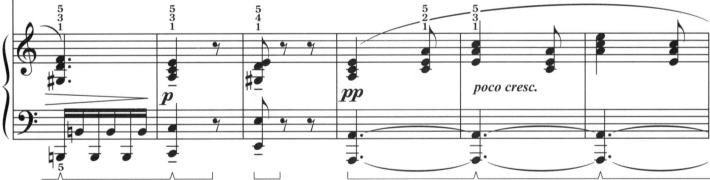

Use with
MORE FAVORITE CLASSICS
Solo Book Two,
page 16.

Sonatina in G Major

Ludwig van Beethoven
(1770–1827)

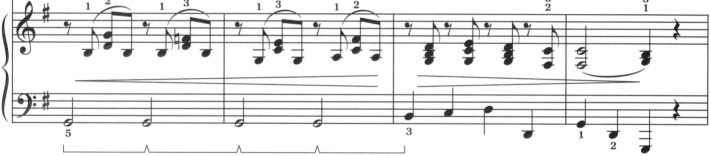

Use with
MORE FAVORITE CLASSICS
Solo Book Two,
page 18.

ROMANZE

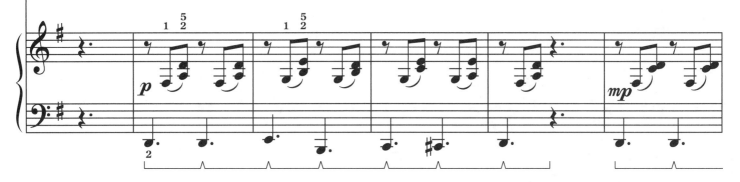

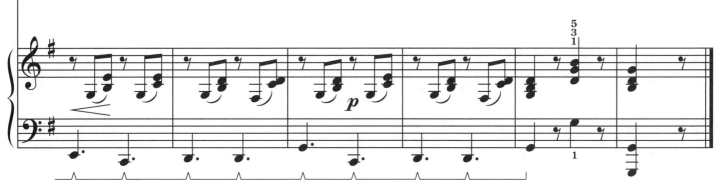

Use with
MORE FAVORITE CLASSICS
Solo Book Two,
page 20.

Sonatina in C Major

Friedrich Kuhlau (1786–1823)
Op. 55, No. 3

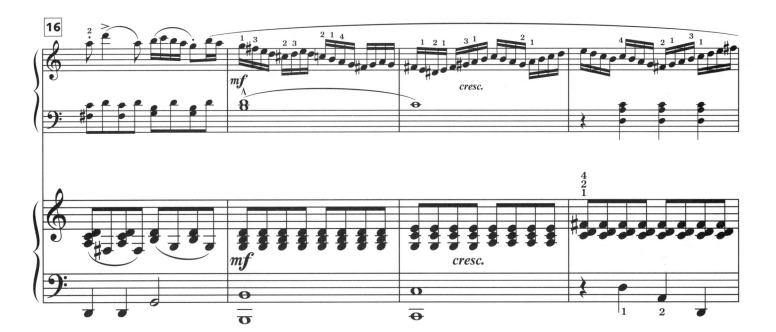

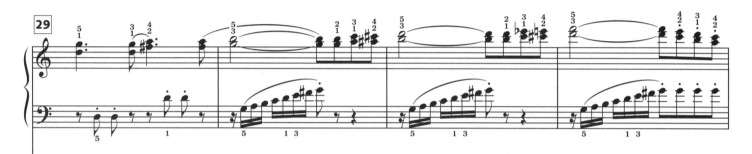

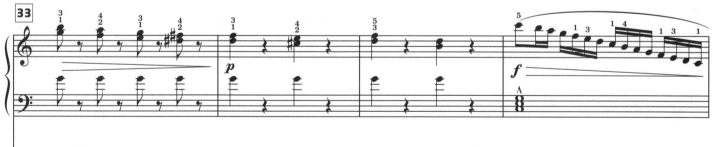

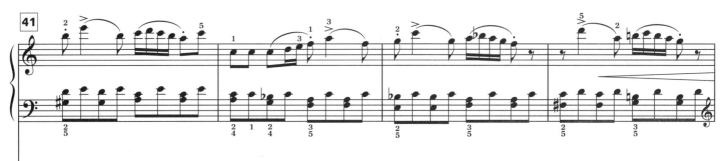

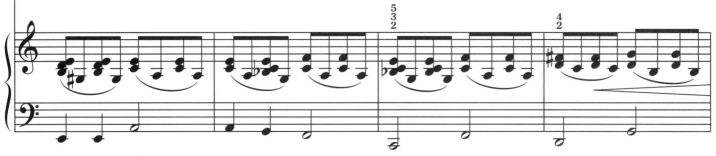

Use with
MORE FAVORITE CLASSICS
Solo Book Two,
page 24.

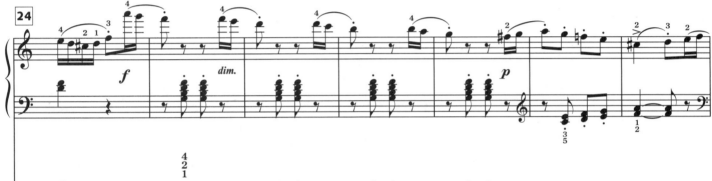

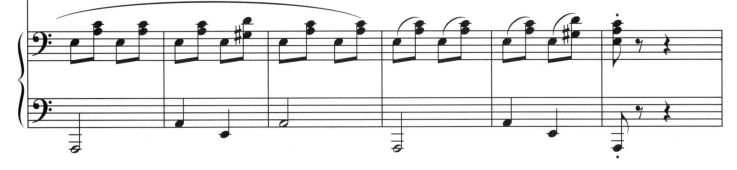

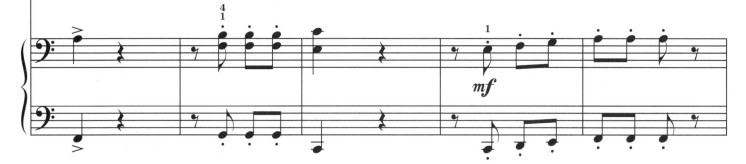

Sonata in C Major
(First Movement)

Wolfgang Amadeus Mozart (1756–1791)
K. 545
Second Part by Edvard Grieg (1843–1907)

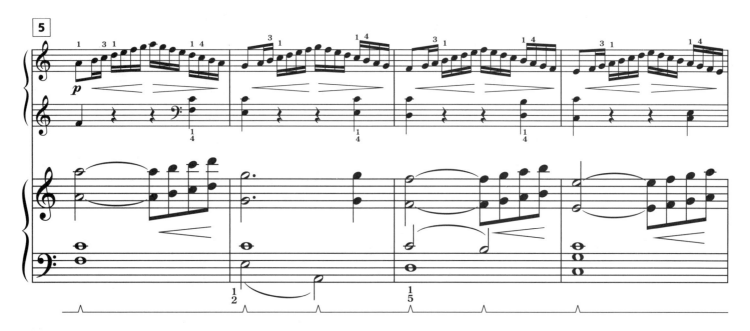

* Pianists with small hands may omit the top note of the LH in measures 9, 22–23, 26–31, 33–35, 54, 67–68, 71–73.

** Pianists with small hands should play only the LH half notes on beats 1 and 3 of measures 18–21 and 63–66.

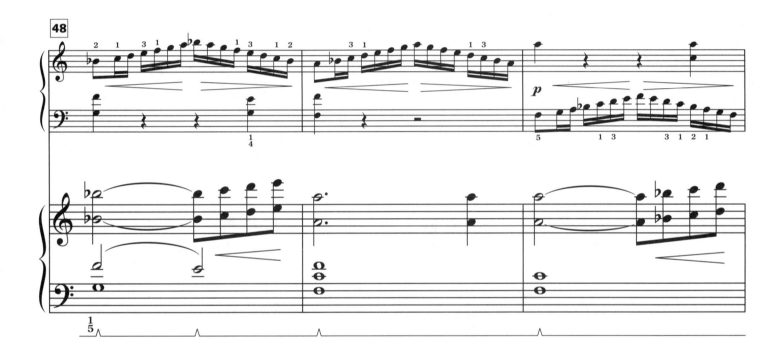

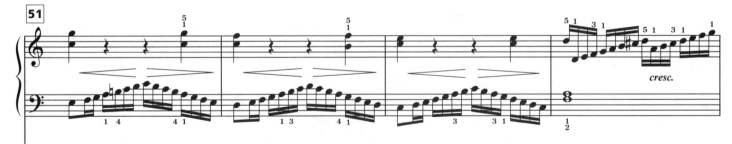

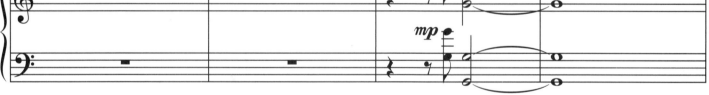

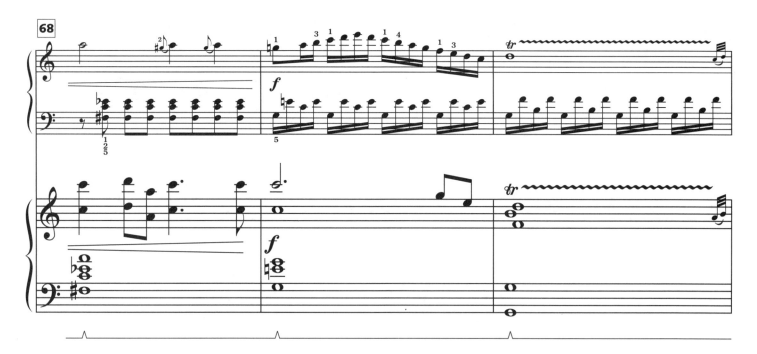

Witches' Dance

Theodor Kullak (1818–1882)
Op. 4, No. 2

Use with
MORE FAVORITE CLASSICS
Solo Book Two,
page 34.

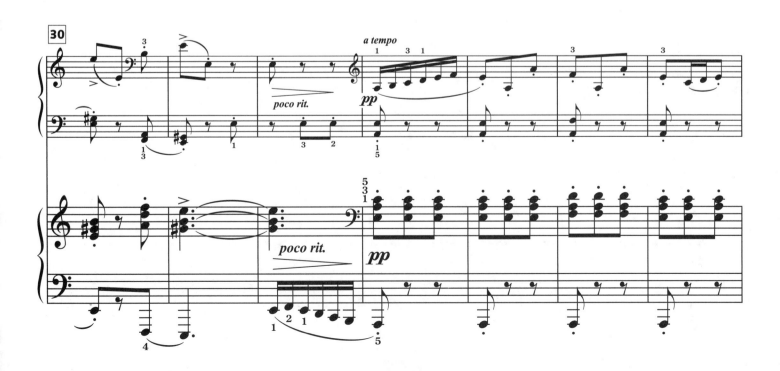

Use with
MORE FAVORITE CLASSICS
Solo Book Two,
page 36.

About Strange Lands and People

(Scenes from Childhood)

Robert Schumann (1810–1856)
Op. 15, No. 1

Use with
MORE FAVORITE CLASSICS
Solo Book Two,
page 38.

Prelude in E Minor

Frédéric François Chopin (1810–1849)
Op. 28, No. 4

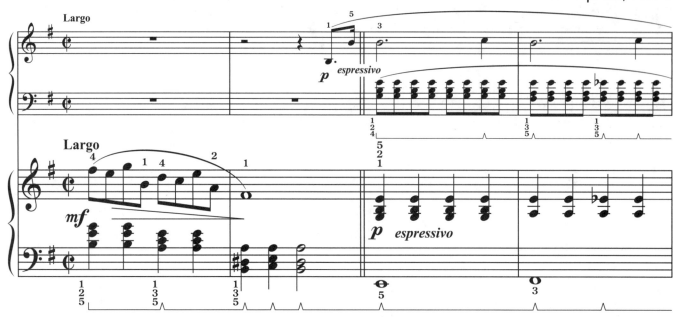

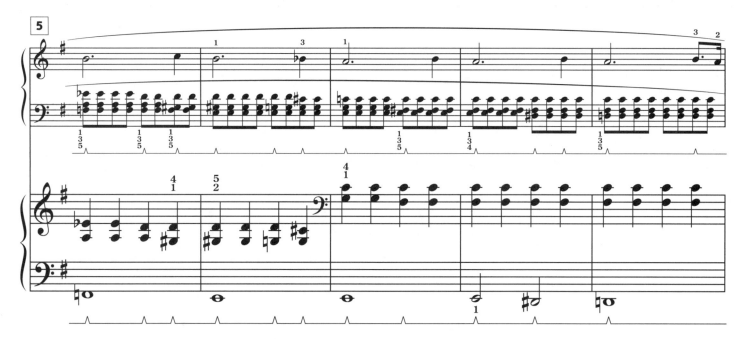

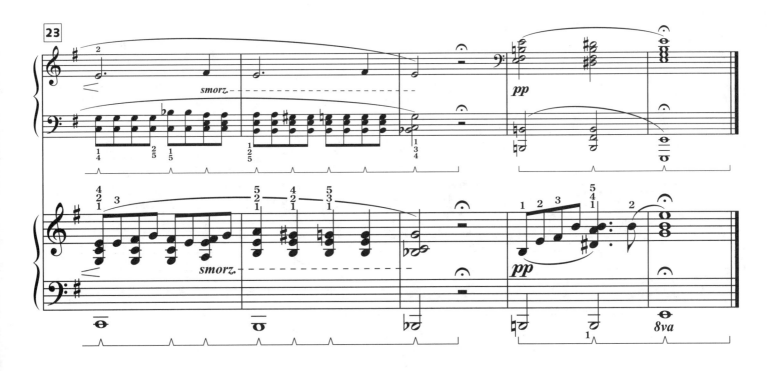

Use with
MORE FAVORITE CLASSICS
Solo Book Two,
page 40.

Prelude in C Minor

Frédéric François Chopin (1810–1849)
Op. 28, No. 20

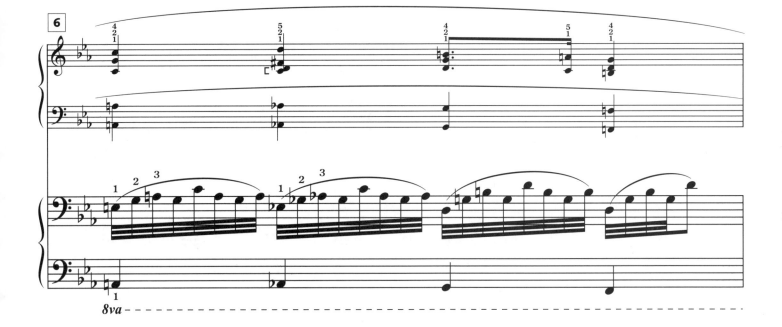

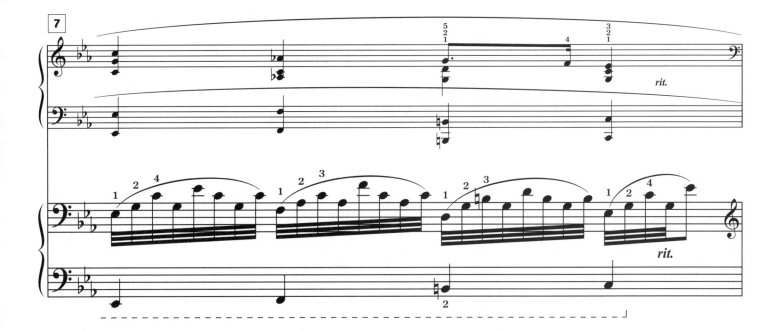

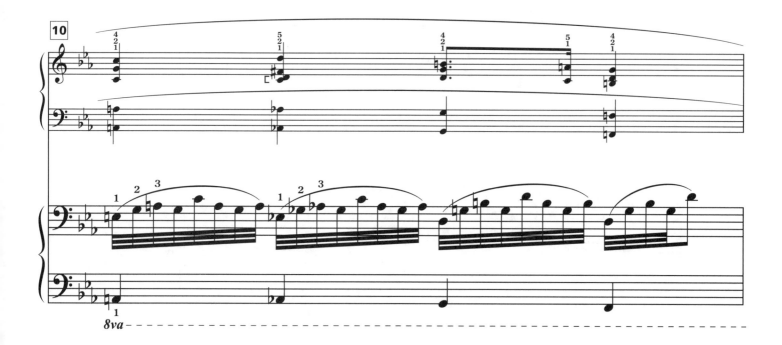

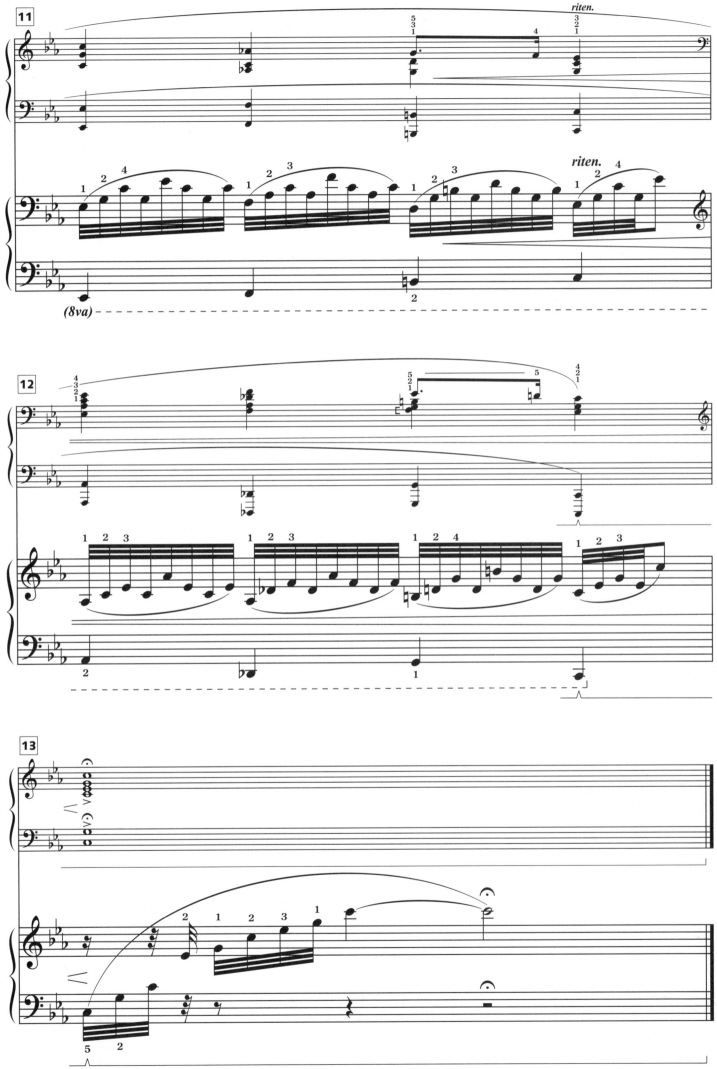

Use with
MORE FAVORITE CLASSICS
Solo Book Two,
page 41.

Waltz in A Minor

Frédéric François Chopin (1810–1849)
Op. Posthumous

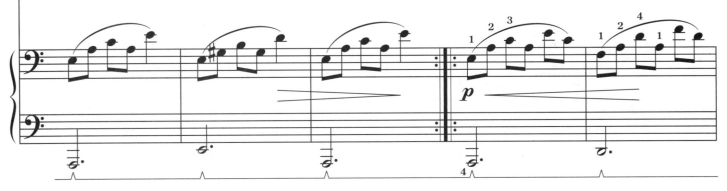

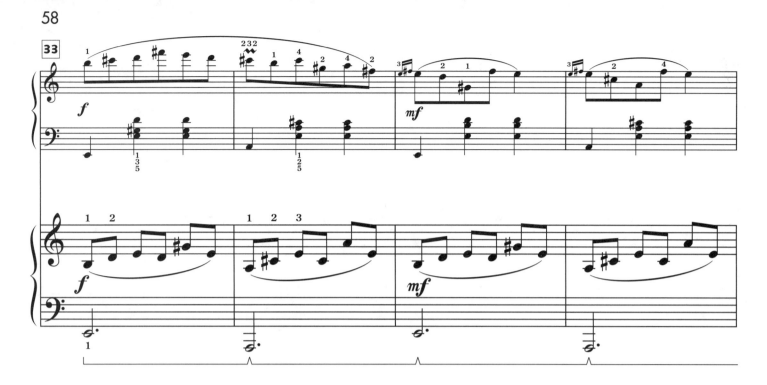

Fluttering Leaves

Use with
MORE FAVORITE CLASSICS
Solo Book Two,
page 44.

Carl Kölling (1831–1914)
Op. 147, No. 2

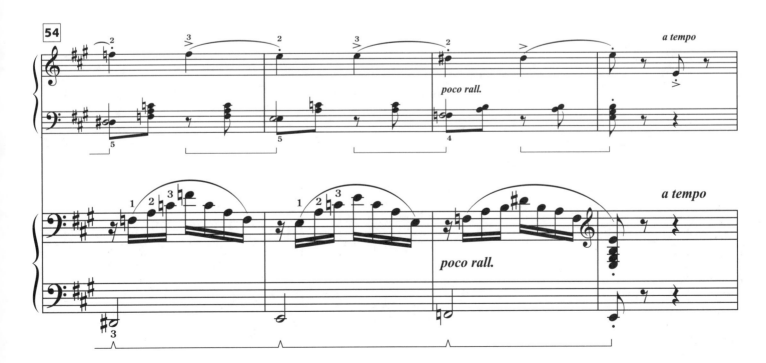

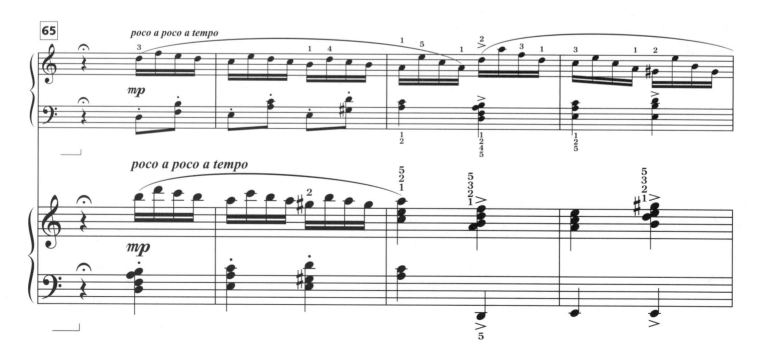

Use with
MORE FAVORITE CLASSICS
Solo Book Two,
page 48.

Venetian Boat Song

(Songs without Words)

Felix Mendelssohn (1809–1847)
Op. 19, No. 6

Use with
MORE FAVORITE CLASSICS
Solo Book Two,
page 50.

Bagatelle

Alexander Tcherepnin (1899–1977)
Op. 5, No. 1

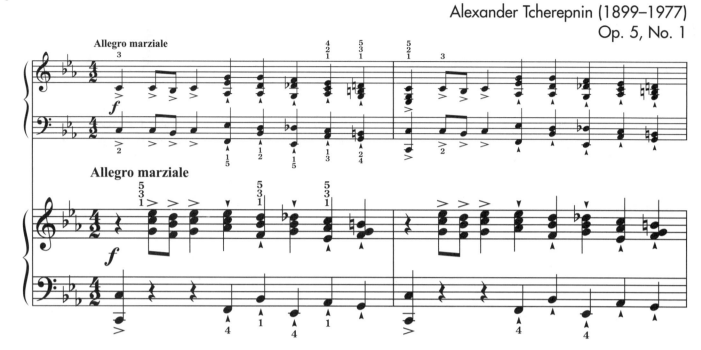

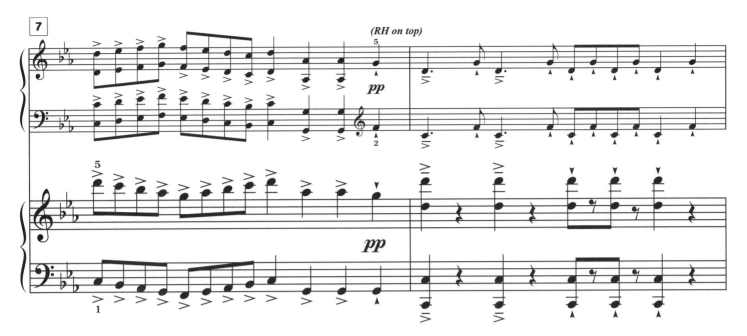

A Giddy Girl
(Histoires)

Use with
MORE FAVORITE CLASSICS
Solo Book Two,
page 52.

Jacques Ibert
(1890–1962)

Allant
dans un style de romance sentimentale anglaise

Allant (going)
dans un style de romance sentimentale anglaise
(in the style of a sentimental English romance)

un peu retenu

au mouvᵗ

un peu retenu (a little ritard.)

au mouvᵗ (a tempo)

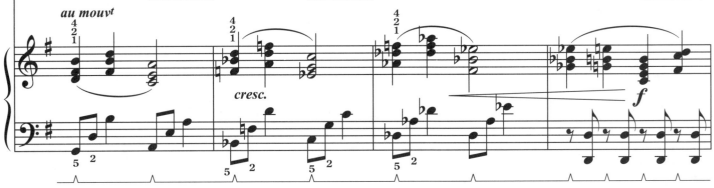

Use with
MORE FAVORITE CLASSICS
Solo Book Two,
page 54.

The Little White Donkey

(Histoires)

Jacques Ibert
(1890–1962)

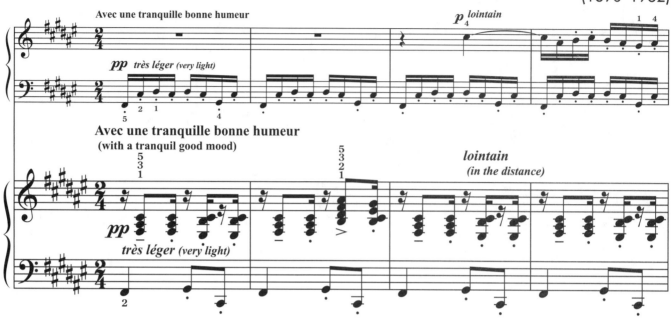

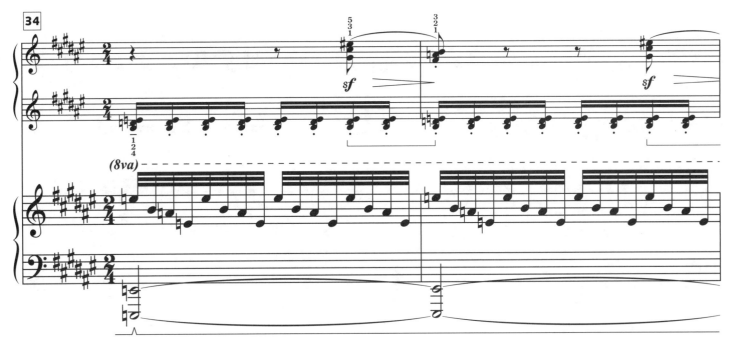

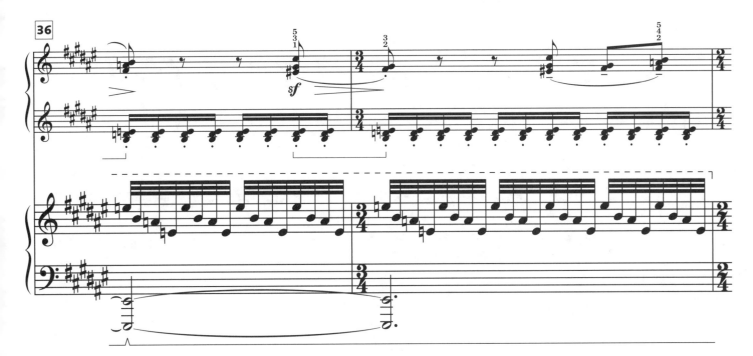

en exagérant un peu les accents
(exaggerate the accents a little)

Un peu ralenti
(a little slower)

Avec la même humeur paisible du début
(with the same peaceful mood as at the beginning)

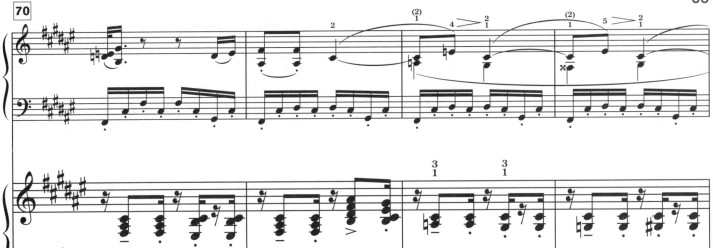

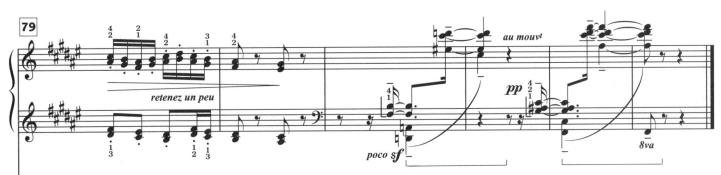

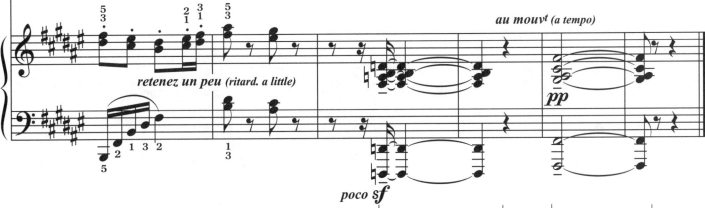

Use with
MORE FAVORITE CLASSICS
Solo Book Two,
page 60.

Golliwogg's Cakewalk
(Children's Corner Suite)

Claude Debussy
(1862–1918)

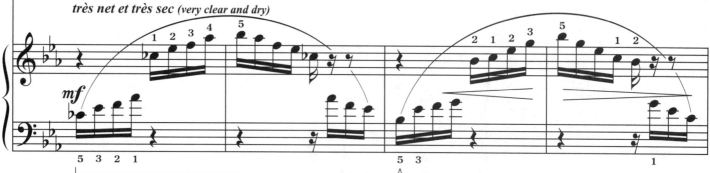

Cédez, avec une grande émotion
(slower, with great emotion)

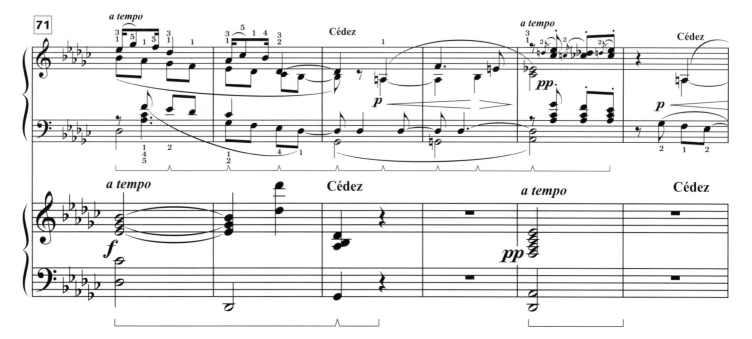

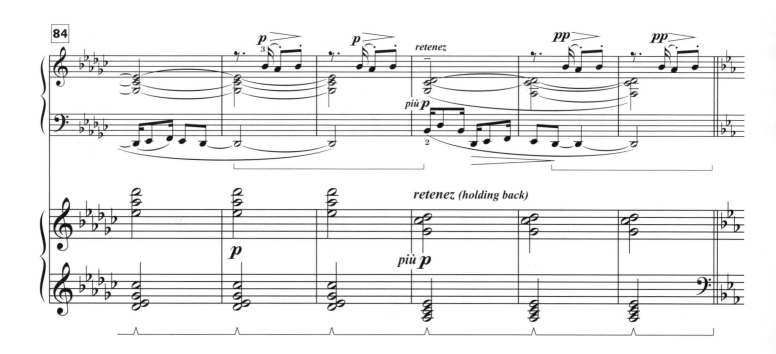

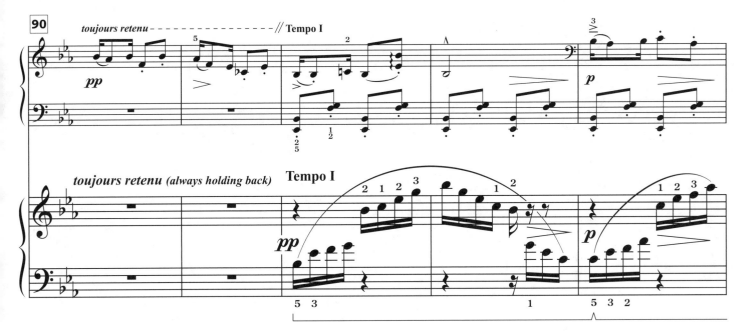